A Biblical Worldview on Sexuality

© Copyright 2024 – Andrew Wommack

Printed in the United States of America. All rights reserved. No portion of this book may be reproduced, stored in a retrieval system, or transmitted in any form or by any means—electronic, mechanical, photocopy, recording, scanning, or other—except for brief quotations in critical reviews or articles, without the prior written permission of the publisher.

Unless otherwise indicated, all Scripture quotations are taken from the New King James Version®. Copyright © 1982 by Thomas Nelson. Used by permission. All rights reserved.

Published in partnership between Andrew Wommack Ministries and Harrison House Publishers.

Woodland Park, CO 80863 – Shippensburg, PA 17257

ISBN 13 TP: 978-1-59548-642-4

For Worldwide Distribution, Printed in the USA

1 2 3 4 5 6 / 26 25 24

CONTENTS

Introduction 1

Chapter 1 The Need for a Biblical Worldview on Sexuality by Alex McFarland 3

Chapter 2 The Purpose and Covenant of Marriage by Duane Sheriff 9

Chapter 3 Sexual Purity by Mike and Carrie Pickett 13

Chapter 4 Adultery, Divorce, and Remarriage by Greg Mohr 19

Chapter 5 The Real Agenda by William J. "Bill" Federer 25

Chapter 6 Homosexuality by Andrew Wommack 31

Chapter 7 Transgenderism by Mike and Carrie Pickett 35

Chapter 8 Tolerance and Love by Andrew Wommack 39

Conclusion 43

Continue Building Your Biblical Worldview 45

Receive Jesus as Your Savior 47

Receive the Holy Spirit 49

Note: This booklet is just a brief introduction to twelve hours of teaching from the Biblical Worldview: Sexuality *curriculum. Statistics included in the **"Did You Know?"** and text sections of this booklet were cited when the complete curriculum was originally published and may no longer represent the most current information.*

About a Biblical Worldview

Everyone views the world based on their beliefs—it's their worldview. As you process everything that you encounter, whether you know it or not, you are looking at it through a lens based on a variety of influences. You filter life based on experiences and factors from your background, such as where you grew up, family dynamics, ethnic heritage, religious upbringing, education and educators' views shared with students, and political views. Every day, your worldview guides your thoughts, decisions, and conversations.

It may surprise you to know that Christians don't automatically have a biblical worldview. When you became a Christian, you just began a journey to renew your mind. You did not automatically get a biblical worldview download at salvation. The problem many Christians face is a clash of worldviews. Often, it is difficult to recognize the daily assault on their Christian values and biblical teachings. Take note the next time you hear a news report or people sharing their perspectives and if you feel a twinge inside that indicates something isn't sitting right in your spirit. Typically, people are busy and ignore that twinge. When someone regularly encounters and hears perspectives that conflict with God's truth, that person can become dulled to it and simply begin to accept those perspectives as truth.

INTRODUCTION

In a society where lawlessness and anarchy have emerged, our culture is bent on defending the stance of "anything goes" when it comes to sexuality. Promiscuity, a disregard for monogamy or traditional family values, and most forcefully, the LGBTQ+ propaganda, are being pushed on us everywhere: government properties fly rainbow flags, schools include transgenderism in their curriculum, children's movies and media promote nonbinary characters, and even retail store giants openly support these agendas—devoting product lines to carry them out. As these messages get more daring and blatantly inconsistent with what the Bible says, it becomes imperative for Christians to speak up.

What should Christians say or do? Aren't Christians supposed to just love and accept everyone? Yes, however, we are especially supposed to speak the truth—in love and with boldness. By building an arsenal of biblical principles with the teaching in this booklet, you will be prepared to speak that truth. Honestly, the most loving thing you can do is to tell someone the truth that will help set them free.

This booklet guides you to discern between what the Bible says and today's popular narrative about sexuality. In a broken world of hurting people, lives destroyed, and futures squandered through the misuse of sex, God has a roadmap for the right way to live. When Christians follow God's roadmap, it will help lead them and then lead others to understand truth about sexuality.

As Christians develop a strong understanding of what God says versus what the world says, they can use truth to begin to deflate the lies and save people from going down the destructive road built by evil agendas. It is time to take territory for the kingdom of heaven by helping people see the light of God's truth about sexuality. It's crucial that we discover the truth ourselves and then help others see it before it's too late.

CHAPTER 1

THE NEED FOR A BIBLICAL WORLDVIEW ON SEXUALITY

by Alex McFarland

Fluidity is a term frequently used nowadays alongside *gender* by people who believe they can pick and choose their gender day-by-day. Many people also ascribe fluidity to their morals. This popular trend frees people to make up what is right and wrong for them. But the truth is we don't get to make our own morals or truth. Despite all of the attempts to legitimize deviancy and all of the arguments and semantical gymnastics that try to defend what we know is wrong, everybody—even the most passionate secularist—knows right from wrong. God's Word definitively states that right and wrong are written on both the hearts of believers in Christ and nonbelievers (Rom. 2:14–15).

Right and wrong give way to a stable society, and the building block of a stable society is the traditional family. The natural home consists of a marriage—a husband and a wife—and children. Nowadays, everything is up for grabs, and people want to reinvent everything. If you advocate for traditional, heterosexual monogamy—one man married to one woman—you'll be scorned.

How did we arrive at this place of moral decline? It's crept into many areas of society, particularly in universities. Nowadays, many college professors are atheists and agnostics and seem to delight in prompting students to question not only the Bible and Christianity, but the very idea that God exists. Here we are in the 21st century, and so much of secular education, Hollywood, media experts, celebrities, and other influencers approach life from a decidedly non-biblical worldview. This has resulted in our culture teetering on the brink of anarchy. We're seeing pockets of lawlessness erupt in America as well as in parts of Europe, which is about fifty years ahead of us in its erosion of Christianity. Frankly, it's the abandonment of God. But for the last 240 years, even the non-Christian Americans—the unchurched—still had a basic moral awareness. They believed in right and wrong and moral truth, but it's not like that today.

Much of our culture has turned away from God—turned away from the idea that there is absolute truth, right and wrong, and morality and immorality. The belief that nothing is immoral affects people's view of beauty, truth, literature, and music. When someone praises an action or condemns an action, the person speaks from a worldview that acknowledges there is an ultimate standard of goodness, truth, beauty, virtue, and love. The highest superlatives—goodness, love, and truth—are embodied in God. So, when we say, "Billy Graham and Mother Teresa were good," what we're actually saying is their life, their words, and their actions were closer to an ultimate objective standard of truth than something else. Contrast that with the names "Adolf Hitler," or "Osama bin Laden," or "terrorism," and "genocide," these have a bad or negative connotation and are far from the standard of goodness or truth.

The only way that we can meaningfully say anything is good or bad is if there's an objective, unchanging standard from which we measure. In fact, we can only discern goodness, truth versus evil, and noise if there's an objective, ultimate standard that never changes. It's the eternal God that we measure against. Before we throw out God, truth, morality, beauty, justice, and virtue, ask yourself: do you really want a world where an Adolf Hitler is no different than a Mother Teresa? That's what we would have.

Today's secular worldview has drifted so far from the good, the true, the virtuous, and the beautiful that we're almost unshockable. People argue for moral relativism by saying sex outside of marriage, abortion, and homosexuality aren't wrong because they don't want to answer to God for their behavior. These same people will then say they don't believe in God because there's evil, terrorism, murder, and violence in the world. But they can't have it both ways. If people throw away morals to pursue any sexual tendency, there will be consequences. It didn't take people long in the 19th century to recognize that if there was no creator in our past, then there will be no judge in our future. The reality is that if God is not part of our origin, God is not part of our destiny; and if God is not the creator of life, then God is not the foundation for morality.

Here we are in the 21st century—nearly two centuries removed from the introductions of evolution and relativism, which have not only reached our schools and education, but they're now even influencing churches. People are morally drifting and asking, "If God is real, why is there evil and injustice, murder, and terrorism in the world?" It's because Satan could not kill God, so he's tried to harm, dehumanize, deface, and devalue the people made in God's image. Today, Satan continues attacking those made in God's image through human trafficking, slavery, and pornography. These topics affect the secular person and should compel them to preserve a Christian worldview because Christianity and moral absolutism elevate the human condition. The human heart is full of darkness. Jeremiah 17:9 says, *"The heart is deceitful above all things, and desperately wicked; who can know it?"*

In other words, we don't even have the capacity to comprehend our own capability for iniquity. That's why we so desperately need to be born again, led by the Spirit, and cleave to Christ every day because the human heart is capable of great wickedness apart from God. Now, more than ever, it is vital to be biblically informed, socially savvy, and culturally engaged as you live to promote truth—especially the truth about sexuality.

CHAPTER 2

THE PURPOSE AND COVENANT OF MARRIAGE

by Duane Sheriff

Imagine being on a construction site where a nail needs to be hammered into a large piece of wood. The contractor looks around for a hammer, the tool designed for the job, but there is only a guitar nearby. Now, if the contractor didn't understand the purpose of the guitar, he could pick up the guitar and pound the nail and finally get it into the wood, but that would be abusing (or would break) the guitar. The purpose of the guitar is to produce beautiful sounds, not to pound in nails. In other words, if you don't know the purpose of something—whatever it is, you're going to be confused, frustrated, and unintentionally abuse it. Ecclesiastes 3:1 tells us, *"To everything* there is *a season, a time for every purpose under heaven."* Everything has a purpose, and marriage is no different.

God created marriage, and like any creation—whether of God or of man, it's the creator who knows the purpose of His creation. A creation doesn't know its purpose; the creator knows. Because marriage was God's idea, we would be wise to learn what His purpose is for marriage. We must know how to discern when we are believing a lie that abuses and counterfeits God's plan. Satan has skillfully caused people—through divorce, sexual immorality, and the confusion of the genders—to have a distorted picture of marriage.

> **DID YOU KNOW?**
> Marriage was created as an institution before the government was created, before Israel was created, and before the church was created. It's the oldest institution known to man, and it was created by God.

God joined male and female in a mystery called marriage (Mark 10:2–9). Female was taken out of Adam. God made woman from Adam and brought her back to him. Female was created on the inside of the first male. In other words, God created them as one, male and female. Then God brought them together. In marriage, they were to be as one as they were in creation.

The purpose of marriage isn't for a man and a woman to come under one roof with two different visions or directions for their life, two different bank accounts, and to live self-centered or with dreams independent of a covenant partner. Part of the purpose of marriage is to no longer live as two but as one flesh (Gen. 2:19–25).

If God had a specific purpose for marriage, that also means there are things He *didn't* create marriage for. He did not create marriage to be a social experiment of male and male together or female and female together. God is the author of our gender, and that's one of the reasons there's such a resistance to gender. One of the ultimate ways to rebel against God is to claim that "no one is going to tell me who or what I am." But Genesis 1:27 says that God made them male and female. It is sad that we live in a culture where it's controversial to say there are only two genders and that God created our gender. God formed us in our mother's womb according to Psalm 139:13–16, so even the gender confusion is an attack on the institution of marriage.

God intended the sacredness and beauty of sex to be experienced through the covenant of marriage. It's not just living together, a partnership, or some contract that you can easily get out of. God joins people together in marriage where the two literally become one. Jesus said in Mark 10:9, *"Therefore what God has joined together, let not man separate."* When God made Adam and Eve one in the covenant of marriage, they were no longer two. On the sixth day of creation, God made male and female on the inside of Adam (Gen. 5:1-2). This is why a man leaves his father and mother and cleaves to his wife (Gen. 2:24). Men should not live two separate lives, but a man should cleave to his wife and form a new family, a new home, and a new place of authority that hadn't been there before.

God revealed through Israel and through His Word that marriage isn't just a contract, not just a piece of paper, and not just sex. Sex is a vital part of the love for each other, and the biblical worldview affirms that sex is to be enjoyed within the boundaries of marriage. He created the institution of marriage and honors the covenant of marriage. That's why we need to learn God's purpose for marriage and teach it to our children before they enter into marriage.

CHAPTER 3
SEXUAL PURITY
by Mike and Carrie Pickett

God is absolutely for the success of your covenant marriage relationship and for the enjoyment of your sexuality. God's not trying to hold anything back from us. He's simply trying to teach us how to live better, more satisfied, and fulfilled lives in every area—including sexuality.

God talks about the sexuality between the man and the woman. Every answer that you need from the Word of God about sexuality takes you back to the original design. Man and woman were created as separate sexes and then came together as one (Gen. 2:24). God actually founded sex before sin came into the world. Sex is not just between the man and the woman—God is involved in the process. There's an anointing to experience all the blessings that God has for you. There's a blessing of multiplication in the area of sexuality because there's expression, joy, freedom, and worship. Go back to God's original intent for a husband and wife in a sexual relationship—it actually becomes worship to God. What an incredible gift God has given us, to be fruitful through sex (Gen. 1:28).

God will not be involved in non-marital intimacy because He has created boundaries. Those boundaries are not there to hinder us—they are there because God loves us. Sin entered into the world, and therefore people started wandering outside the boundaries God established. Today, sexually transmitted diseases happen when someone wanders outside the borders that God has created. Satan takes advantage of this because his only goal is to steal, kill, and destroy (John 10:10). He is always looking for a counterfeit and for ways to sabotage something that God originally created. Sexuality is supposed to be a beautiful picture of God's deep intimacy with us, where we can be totally open and in love with Him, knowing that He absolutely loves us unconditionally.

The boundaries of sex that the world is trying to establish are different from God's boundaries, and they're very confusing. The secular worldview says that as long as it feels right and it's not causing a problem for other people, then it's perfectly acceptable. The reality is that God gave us boundaries so we would have success in everything we do. He wants us to have prosperous and fulfilled lives through the process of intimacy, which He's created within the boundaries of marriage. God created sex and marriage, and He established this as His framework. Inside of this framework, it's going to be beautiful. The enemy seeks to take sex outside of that frame, and in doing so, it becomes chaotic, full of confusion, and full of shame. Within the context of marriage, you can have a sexual relationship and unity, and it is not shameful. Before marriage or outside of marriage, it's shameful.

Today, many people engage in premarital sex, and it skews their opinions of what intimacy actually looks like. Then, when they enter into marriage, they find it more difficult to connect with their spouse and stay together during difficult times. Prior to getting married, they had sex with somebody else, and then each went their own way.

Adultery is often given a nicer image and called a love affair. Adultery says, "If it's just not working, and you fall out of love, it's okay to fall in love with someone else, even while you're still married." But it is the ultimate betrayal of the marriage covenant relationship.

The true purpose of marriage is to serve one another in an intimate relationship. But the enemy is trying to get your attention off of that and get you to only think about yourself. That's one of the reasons why pornography is a thriving internet industry. The enemy will take a craving and make it lust, and then boundaries will be crossed.

Now pornography has moved in the direction of adults seeking out children. The enemy is not just trying to draw adults into pornography; he is trying to bring young people into these temptations. Many young men and young women get introduced to pornography at a young age. It is presented as just something so casual and normal but creates curiosity. We have to aggressively recognize that we cannot accept this worldview. We must tell our children that this is not acceptable, normal, or healthy, and that they can't have this freedom in sexuality.

There are many sexual distractions because the enemy knows that if he can get your mind and attention off the true focus of the Word, you're

> **DID YOU KNOW?**
>
> Pornography actually reshapes the way people think.[1] It trains people to be stimulated by a certain set of parameters that are outside of a real personal relationship. People get trained to look at a screen, and it is rewiring the brain to feed the addiction of that process—to keep the addict coming back for more.

rendered powerless to resist him and powerless to walk after what the Spirit of God has planned for you. The enemy is lying about sexuality. We need to get back to the beauty of what God created so that we know how to protect and have a healthy sexuality.

CHAPTER 4

ADULTERY, DIVORCE, AND REMARRIAGE

by Greg Mohr

Adultery is first mentioned in the Bible as one of the Ten Commandments, *"You shall not commit adultery"* (Ex. 20:14). It may surprise you to learn that it's a sin against God because it's a failure to trust Him to meet your needs in this area of marriage, which He created. God created your sexuality and ordained that it be fulfilled inside the boundaries of a healthy marriage relationship. Sexual sin affects your relationship with God; but also on a horizontal plane, it affects and hurts people around you. It hurts your spouse, your children, your family and other relationships. The Bible talks about not getting involved in adultery and fornication because they are sin against your body (1 Thess. 4:3–4); and it's sin that hurts the spiritual body of Christ like none other.

> **DID YOU KNOW?**
> Adultery never starts physically. It always starts emotionally. In order for an emotional connection to start somewhere else, there has to be an emotional disconnection in your present marriage relationship.

There are usually warning signs that someone is vulnerable to adultery. For believers, it starts with a lack of intimacy with God. John 8:31-32 shows that if we continue in His Word, we'll be His disciples, and we'll know the truth, and the truth will set us free. John 15:5 says, *"I am the vine, you are the branches. He who abides in Me, and I in him, bears much fruit; for without Me you can do nothing."* According to this verse, we are to bear fruit. Violating our covenant of marriage doesn't bear fruit, and it certainly isn't freedom or a sign of discipleship. You can't go out and commit adultery when you have intimacy with the Lord. God wants to show you how to minister to your mate. So, guard your intimacy with the Lord.

In Mark 10:2-12, the Pharisees came to Jesus and asked if they could use the Law of Moses to write a divorce decree for any reason. Jesus revealed that the law was written because of the hardness of their hearts (Mark 10:5). Their selfishness—and allowing distance in their relationship with their mate—opened the door to adultery and other things. So, don't allow emotional space to separate your relationship with your spouse. Another sign of being vulnerable to adultery is a wounded heart (Prov. 7:26). If you've gone through betrayal, hurt, loss, or disappointment, your heart is vulnerable for someone to flatter you and try to minister to you.

When Jesus addressed divorce and the hardness in the hearts of the Pharisees (Matt. 19:1– 10), they basically asked if they could trade in their wives for "newer models." They were looking for a loophole in the Law and tried to get Jesus to reinforce it. The grass looked greener on the other side, but He put the responsibility right back on these guys for the condition of their marriage relationships. Jesus pointed out that even if they got a divorce and then remarried, they already had adultery in their hearts. The divorce wasn't going to remove it.

Many Christians view remarriage as adultery based on Mark 10:11–12, *"Whoever divorces his wife and marries another commits adultery against her. And if a woman divorces her husband and marries another, she commits adultery."* I don't believe that Jesus is saying if someone gets divorced and if they ever remarry, they're committing adultery. First of all, in order to commit adultery, you have to be married. If you're divorced, you're not married. If you're involved intimately with someone after you're divorced, that's fornication—not adultery.

Another marriage-related topic addressed in the Bible is separation. The apostle Paul gave the biblical reason for a husband and wife to separate only for the purpose of reconciliation, not for the purpose of divorce and remarriage (1 Cor. 7:10-11). Paul and Jesus were basically saying the same thing by forbidding divorce for convenience.

We do live in a fallen world. As a pastor, I've dealt with terrible and heart-wrenching situations of families that were broken up by physical abuse, violence, or because one of the spouses molested the children. Certainly, there are situations where you have to remove the family member from that person until they can be trusted again.

The bottom line is that no matter who is at fault in a divorce—God's not angry with you. He hates divorce. He hates the impact that it has on others, but He's not angry with you. He's not binding you up or putting you under the scourge of calling you an adulterer. If you're already divorced or widowed, it's not a sin to remarry. When you understand the truth of what the Bible says about adultery, divorce, and remarriage, then you won't believe the lies from the enemy who comes to steal, kill, and destroy (John 10:10). Let the Word of God set free you, release you from shame, and bring healing to your heart.

CHAPTER 5
THE REAL AGENDA
by William J. "Bill" Federer

The liberal sexual agenda is a relatively recent development. Like water trickling through a levy and then suddenly bursting into a flood, the sexual transformation began slowly, then increased at an accelerating speed. It's moving in a direction that is so far from biblical morality, which says that God made every individual male and female in His image. But in a mysterious and wonderful way, a man and a woman united in marriage also reflects the image of God. Thus, at some level, the attack on two sexes and on marriage is an attack on the very image of God.

There's a subjective invention of the difference between sex and gender: sex being biological and gender being subjective and fluid, based on your feelings. Instead of teaching children that there are absolutes, they're taught it's all about their feelings—doing what feels right. But the Gospel teaches us to renew our minds (Rom. 12:2) and to take control of our thoughts and feelings (2 Cor. 10:5). However, this new sexual agenda teaches a belief system that your feelings control and define you. Feelings change every day, and so sexual identity can change every day. To add to the confusion, if you don't address someone according to the gender they "feel like," with the right pronoun, you're considered hateful.

This secular sexual agenda begins when impressionable youth are indoctrinated with alternative sexual arrangements. Hollywood presents characters in movies and in sitcoms who are gay or have alternative sexual identities. Even more recently (as of this writing), the agenda has moved from gay marriage to transgenderism. A dozen years ago, in almost the entire population of America, no one had heard of the term *transgender*; but suddenly, it has become mainstream.

But there is an even larger agenda, and the first step in that agenda involves teaching the LGBTQ agenda in schools. This produces lawless students with no concept of right or wrong and no absolutes because they're ruled by their feelings. Lawlessness has influenced some students to act out what they've been taught and even justified killing classmates. After all, they believe everyone evolved from a swamp, and there's no purpose to life. The result? Society embraces lawlessness, and there's an insecurity for life and property; but many people begin to call for a strong power to restore order. The truth is, removing moral restraints leads to more crime, which leads to more government. This will allow an elite ruling class to seize power. Then a party boss will take enough power and become a dictator. The world saw this in 1934, when Hitler used a group of societal outcasts called Brown Shirts to spread violence.[2] Once Hitler seized power, he executed the Brown Shirts in the Night of the Long Knives. He used them, then arose as the dictator.

History shows that when Hitler or anyone devalues human life, there is a domino effect. Look at how sexual sin leads to an unwanted pregnancy and then abortion. Subsequently, whenever the value of human life is decreased, crime increases; and more crime leads to the insecurity of life and property. Then this leads to a cry for a stronger government to restore order. The government ends up taking away freedoms, guns, and all these rights. Eventually, the result is a totalitarian dictatorship.

> **Did You Know?**
>
> There are three main strategies used to promote an agenda:
>
> 1. *Psychological projection*: accusing someone else of what you really are, e.g., rude people who call those they don't like rude.
> 2. *Victimhood*: the aggressor claims to be the victim to justify their own aggression.
> 3. *Seizing the moral high ground*: corrupt leaders wanting to appear righteous.

The LGBTQ agenda opposes a biblical worldview and is a declaration of war on the Gospel. If the government can declare that sin is no longer sin, then obviously you do not need a Savior to wash you from your sins (Rev. 1:5). Despite this moral war, Muslims, Hindus, Buddhists, and other native religions have joined Christians and Jews in believing that there are only two genders: man and woman. At the same time, the government today is stepping into the realm of theology and forcing people to change their religious beliefs, or the government will come after you.

This liberal agenda is no longer just in government, public schools, Hollywood, or the media. It's now coming into the churches. These people are not content with having their activity; they want to force traditionalists to validate them. They're not content with coming out of the closet; they want to shove you into it. And if you are silent, knowing all that is happening, you are consenting to all of it. Decades ago, the minister officiating a wedding ceremony would say, "If anyone is against this wedding, speak now or forever hold your peace." If you sit there quietly holding your peace, you are consenting to the wedding. Likewise, your silence on these topics of sexuality equals your consent.

Because the church has remained silent, young people aren't standing up for the truth about who God has created them to be. Today's youth face strong motivation to want acceptance in a group. Those pushing the LGBTQ agenda have manipulated this desire to belong and be accepted. In schools, a teacher might ridicule a student for believing it is normal to have a mommy and a daddy. Other students don't want to get yelled at, and so they also ridicule the student. The Bible calls us to stop seeking acceptance by others. We should be content knowing we are accepted by God. We are to love other people, whether they accept us or not. Jesus Himself was rejected. We have to have backbone and declare that we are going to follow God and the Bible—no matter what the world says.

CHAPTER 6
HOMOSEXUALITY
by Andrew Wommack

The ultimate biblical account on homosexuality is in Genesis 19, which chronicles God's punishment of Sodom and Gomorrah. Two angels went to the city of Sodom. Lot, who was Abraham's nephew, invited them into his home. All of the men from every quarter of the city came to the door of Lot's house and said to *"bring them out unto us [these two men], that we may know them"* (Gen. 19:5). The word *know* in Scripture is talking about the most intimate, personal relationship between a husband and his wife; but this verse was referring to homosexuality. The NIV makes it very clear in Genesis 19:5, *"Bring them out to us so that we can have sex with them."* The angel smote all of these men with blindness (v. 11). Then, the angel grabbed hold of Lot's hand, his wife's hand, and his two daughters, and brought them out of the city. As the sun was coming up, God rained fire and brimstone down upon the cities of

> **Did You Know?**
> The word *homosexual* wasn't even created until 1869 in Germany.[3] So of course, the word *homosexuality* isn't used in Scripture.

Sodom and Gomorrah and destroyed all of those people (vv. 15–25).

Second Peter 2:6 also shows how God dealt with homosexuality in Sodom and Gomorrah. The book of Jude says that God set forth the areas of Sodom and Gomorrah as an example suffering the vengeance of eternal fire (Jude 7). According to these scriptures, there is no way to pass over them and say that the Bible condones or allows homosexuality. But Scripture does allow forgiveness; and a person can be forgiven, delivered, and changed from homosexuality. You just cannot use the Bible to verify that homosexuality is a God-approved lifestyle.

The Bible also points out that homosexuality is demonic. When a person yields to homosexuality, they have yielded themselves to the devil. This is demonically inspired. Two men or two women coming together is a lie, and Satan is the author of all lies and the father of all of them (John 8:44). Anything that's contrary to what God says originates with the devil. God created man and woman for marriage and to procreate. A person who has entered into a homosexual relationship/lifestyle has been deceived and under demonic influence (1 Pet. 5:8).

There are also physical and emotional effects of the homosexual lifestyle, more than likely because of the multiple sexual encounters people have. A classic study of male and female homosexuality found that 43 percent of white homosexuals had sex with five hundred or more partners.[4] And on average, a homosexual dies twenty years earlier than their heterosexual counterparts.[5]

From God's perspective, there are no levels of transgressions against God—one sin isn't worse than the other. It doesn't matter how much you've sinned or what you've done. God can forgive homosexuality the same as He can forgive anything else. When people practice a homosexual lifestyle, they have moved into a realm where they have willingly disobeyed and rebelled against God. Under the Old Covenant, God commanded death to the people that had given themselves over to the devil to such a degree that they couldn't be delivered, couldn't be changed, or couldn't be born again. It was like a cancer that, if you didn't deal with it, would spread into the entire society and destroy it. Under the New Covenant, we have been given grace because our punishment has been placed upon Jesus. Some people see grace as a license to sin, but if you have truly received God's grace, you'll want to live a pure and holy life. You won't want to live a sinful life (1 John 3:3). And since Jesus is the cure for all sin, a homosexual can be born again and come out of homosexuality.

God loves the homosexual. Homosexuality has been covered in the atonement of the Lord, and a homosexual can be forgiven and cleansed. However, you cannot justify homosexuality. If you are going to have a biblical worldview on sexuality, then you are going to have to reject homosexuality as a lifestyle—not homosexuals. Christians have the truth (Rom. 8:32), and we need to be speaking out and sharing the biblical view of sexuality.

CHAPTER 7
TRANSGENDERISM
by Mike and Carrie Pickett

The enemy is pushing transgenderism on everyone, especially young people, to believe that their gender doesn't have to match their biological sex. When believers go to the Word of God, their biblical worldview paints a very different picture of the transgender topic. When we talk about transgenderism, we're talking about sin because it is outside of God's original design and plan. God created us in a very specific way—male and female (Gen. 1:27)—because He loved us.

We are going to find the most satisfaction, fulfillment, and purpose when we embrace that God created each and every person with a purpose and with a plan. We are not mistakes (Ps. 139:14–16; Jer. 29:11). Anything we try to accomplish outside of that plan makes it so difficult to succeed. That's why so many people struggle and why the transgender suicide rate is so high.[6]

> **Did You Know?**
>
> The term *transsexual* was first used in 1949 by David Oliver Cauldwell; and in 1966, it was popularized by Harvey Benjamin.[7] The term *transgender* came around the same time.
>
> A Gallup poll in 2016 established that about 0.6 percent of the U.S. population considers themselves transgender, or around 1.4 million people.[8]

When we look back at history, we see erosions of biblical views on sexuality and the effects on people and nations that have led to where society is today. In 1934, Joseph Daniel Unwin published a book called *Sex and Culture*, which looked at over eighty-six different cultures, societies, and civilizations.[9] He looked for patterns within civilizations over a five-thousand-year period. One of Unwin's findings showed that within three generations, the cultures that combined premarital chastity and staying married for the rest of their lives reached the peak in every area of society. When Unwin looked at societies with total sexual freedom, both prior to getting married and also within marriage, he found that they always collapsed within three generations—that's approximately ninety years; and sometimes it was even sooner. If we can understand what has happened in the past, then we can learn from those mistakes and understand that the impact of those mistakes is not just for this generation but for the many generations that are to come.

We see the pattern of the sexual revolution of the '60s and '70s, which promoted sex before marriage and then living with each other outside of marriage, led to higher divorce and abortion rates of the '80s and '90s. In the 1960s, they weren't talking about legalizing their lifestyle choices. But now, if you don't accept these deviant lifestyle choices, then "you're against all of us, and you're against society." The enemy's agenda has been to take us slowly, from generation to generation.

A study in 2020 showed the "most vulnerable to sex denialism is children."[10] Gender identity starts to cause major confusion in children. If a little girl plays with snakes and frogs, then she must really be a little boy. Or a little boy that plays dolls with his sister must really be a girl. The world is really pushing and trying to get children to decide, versus giving them time to reach puberty and get over their hormones. Puberty-blocking drugs and therapies reinforce confusion. This causes the child to question whether he or she is really a boy or a girl.

However, children flourish when they can expect and know what the boundaries are. If people believe there's no right or wrong, then there's no gender; and all of a sudden, there are no boundaries. But we need to realize that the enemy's goal is for normal, sane people—especially the church and believers—to stay quiet and mind their own business. Believers also need to understand these tactics of the enemy because, not only is our culture legalizing and celebrating it, but now they're teaching it in classrooms.

CHAPTER 8
TOLERANCE AND LOVE
by Andrew Wommack

When it comes to the topics dealing with sexuality, any time you start taking a stand on morality and present what the Bible says, people are going to come out against you. They're going to misquote scripture and say that you're intolerant, you're a homophobe, you are judging, and you are spewing "hate speech." They have taken what the Lord said about turning the other cheek and not retaliating (Matt. 5:39) and have scared Christians into staying silent on these moral issues.

If you say that you love a person, how could you not warn them of approaching danger? When people give themselves over to homosexuality, transgenderism, or any issues that are contrary to the Word of God, they have seared their conscience. They have taken away all filters and given the devil access to them that destroys their lives and our society. When you see this happening and you don't take a stand, it means that you are not willing to suffer the potential rejection and criticism of being called a homophobe or a hatemonger. As a result, we have allowed the ungodly to dictate morals.

We are the salt of the earth (Matt. 5:13–14). Salt is a preserving influence, and the reason that our world is becoming increasingly more corrupt and immoral is because the church has not stood up and spoken out. You can't expect the ungodly to come up with godly solutions for problems. The Bible has an answer for every problem that people have. If you don't tell someone the truth, then you've rejected the truth for that person. It's wrong for me to reject the truth for another person. I tell people what I believe the truth is, and if they don't like it, I still love them. I'm not rejecting them, but I am not going to reject the truth for them. I'm going to declare what the Word of God says, and all of these things that the Bible calls abominations or sexual perversions are wrong.

Many Christians don't speak out against sin because they mistakenly believe the Bible teaches tolerance. The Bible does **not** teach tolerance. Jesus made a whip out of cords and went into the temple where people were violating what the true intent of the temple was. He got so angry that He actually whipped people, overturned their tables, and set all of the doves and other animals free, which cost those merchants money (John 2:13–16; Mark 11:15–17). Jesus was not tolerant. He didn't sit there and turn the other cheek or look the other way.

We need to be saying what the Word of God says; and that's not being intolerant—that is true love. What most Christians are calling tolerance is nothing but self-love, the fear of man, or the fear of whatever could come against you. God did not make us to be this way.

You can't truly love a person if you don't hate the evil that is trying to destroy them. If you truly love a person, you're going to tell them the truth. We think that loving other people is always smiling at them and never saying anything that would make them uncomfortable or offend them. That is not love; that is love for yourself. You are operating in a fear of man instead of a fear of God. It's time we stand up and start boldly speaking the Word of God.

CONCLUSION

Sexual confusion and deviancy run rampant because Satan comes to steal, kill, and destroy (John 10:10) what God designed for good. God designed men and women to experience and enjoy His plan and purpose for sexual intimacy in marriage. One of the ways the devil has most effectively harmed the ones made in God's image is by devaluing and dehumanizing God's creation through sexual sin. It's important that we as the body of Christ stand up for God's plan for sexuality, learn to protect and teach our children sexual purity, and guard our own marriages. People have lost sight that marriage is about laying down your own desires and fulfilling the covenant relationship. We need to show a new generation that sexuality is something authentic and genuine, and that marriage beautifully reflects the relationship between Christ and the church.

The bottom line is that God created sexuality and marriage. He gave us the instructions, and we should never deviate from it and exalt our opinion or society's opinion above what God says. It takes backbone to stand up for Jesus and to stand up for the Bible's teachings. We have to be willing to boldly address every issue—including the sexuality issue.

CONTINUE BUILDING YOUR BIBLICAL WORLDVIEW

Every day, you are confronted with non-biblical worldviews coming to you through social media, the internet, and secular news sources. The **Truth and Liberty Coalition** (**www.truthandliberty.net**) can guide you to process current events through the lens of God's Word.

- *Live Call-in Show:* insight on current issues and callers can ask questions about biblical worldview or any topic
- *Website:* resources include a 24/7 news feed, links to other online content related to biblical worldview and current American government issues, blogs, voter guides, and prayer guides

If you enjoyed this booklet and would like more tools to arm yourself with a biblical worldview, I suggest these teachings:

- *Biblical Worldview: Sexuality* (complete curriculum)
- *Relationship University*
- *Biblical Worldview* series
- *Observing All Things*

Some of these teachings are available for free at **awmi.net**, or they can be purchased at **awmi.net/store**.

RECEIVE JESUS AS YOUR SAVIOR

Choosing to receive Jesus Christ as your Lord and Savior is the most important decision you'll ever make!

God's Word promises, *"That if thou shalt confess with thy mouth the Lord Jesus, and shalt believe in thine heart that God hath raised him from the dead, thou shalt be saved. For with the heart man believeth unto righteousness; and with the mouth confession is made unto salvation"* (Rom. 10:9-10). *"For whosoever shall call upon the name of the Lord shall be saved"* (Rom. 10:13). By His grace, God has already done everything to provide salvation. Your part is simply to believe and receive.

Pray out loud: "Jesus, I confess that You are my Lord and Savior. I believe in my heart that God raised You from the dead. By faith in Your Word, I receive salvation now. Thank You for saving me."

The very moment you commit your life to Jesus Christ, the truth of His Word instantly comes to pass in your spirit. Now that you're born again, there's a brand-new you!

Please contact us and let us know that you've prayed to receive Jesus as your Savior. We'd like to send you some free materials to help you on your new journey. Call our Helpline: **719-635-1111** (available 24 hours a day, seven days a week) to speak to a staff member who is here to help you understand and grow in your new relationship with the Lord.

Welcome to your new life!

RECEIVE THE HOLY SPIRIT

As His child, your loving heavenly Father wants to give you the supernatural power you need to live a new life. *"For every one that asketh receiveth; and he that seeketh findeth; and to him that knocketh it shall be opened...how much more shall your heavenly Father give the Holy Spirit to them that ask him?"* (Luke 11:10–13).

All you have to do is ask, believe, and receive!

Pray this: "Father, I recognize my need for Your power to live a new life. Please fill me with Your Holy Spirit. By faith, I receive it right now. Thank You for baptizing me. Holy Spirit, You are welcome in my life."

Some syllables from a language you don't recognize will rise up from your heart to your mouth (1 Cor. 14:14). As you speak them out loud by faith, you're releasing God's power from within and building yourself up in the spirit (1 Cor. 14:4). You can do this whenever and wherever you like.

It doesn't really matter whether you felt anything or not when you prayed to receive the Lord and His Spirit. If you believed in your heart that you received, then God's Word promises you did. *"Therefore I say unto you, What things soever ye desire, when ye pray, believe that ye receive* **them***, and ye shall have* **them**" (Mark 11:24). God always honors His Word—believe it!

We would like to rejoice with you and help you understand more fully what has taken place in your life!

Please contact us to let us know that you've prayed to be filled with the Holy Spirit and to request the book *The New You & the Holy Spirit*. This book will explain in more detail about the benefits of being filled with the Holy Spirit and speaking in tongues. Call our Helpline: **719-635-1111** (available 24 hours a day, seven days a week).

CALL FOR PRAYER

If you need prayer for any reason, you can call our Helpline, 24 hours a day, seven days a week at **719-635-1111**. A trained prayer minister will answer your call and pray with you.

Every day, we receive testimonies of healings and other miracles from our Helpline, and we are ministering God's nearly-too-good-to-be-true message of the Gospel to more people than ever. So, I encourage you to call today!

ABOUT THE AUTHORS

Andrew Wommack

Andrew Wommack's life was forever changed the moment he encountered the supernatural love of God on March 23, 1968. As a renowned Bible teacher and author, Andrew has made it his mission to change the way the world sees God.

Andrew's vision is to go as far and deep with the Gospel as possible. His message goes far through the *Gospel Truth* television program, which is available to over half the world's population. The message goes deep through discipleship at Charis Bible College, headquartered in Woodland Park, Colorado. Founded in 1994, Charis has campuses across the United States and around the globe. Andrew is also the president of the Truth & Liberty Coalition, an organization that seeks to educate, unify, and mobilize believers to impact culture and effect godly change on important social issues.

Andrew also has an extensive library of teaching materials in print, audio, and video. More than 200,000 hours of free teachings can be accessed at **awmi.net**.

Alex McFarland

Alex McFarland is a Christian apologist, author, evangelist, religion and culture analyst, and advocate for biblical truth. He speaks at Christian events, conferences, debates, and other venues to teach biblical truths and preach the Gospel. He has been a spokesperson on Fox News and other media outlets. Alex is the only evangelist to have preached in all fifty states in only fifty days. His "Tour Of Truth" crusade swept across America with sixty-four evangelistic services from which came many decisions to receive Jesus and by which many Christians were equipped and encouraged. Find out more about Alex at **AlexMcFarland.com**.

William J. "Bill" Federer

William J. "Bill" Federer is a nationally known speaker, best-selling author, and president of Amerisearch, Inc., a publishing company dedicated to researching America's noble heritage. Bill's *American Minute* radio feature is broadcast daily across America and on the internet. His *Faith in History* television program airs on the TCT Network and via DirectTV. Find out more about Bill at **AmericanMinute.com**.

Mike and Carrie Pickett

Mike was a missionary in Russia for eleven years before meeting his wife, Carrie, and encountering Charis Bible College for the first time. After having his life transformed by the message of God's love and grace, Mike became an instructor in the school and eventually the director of Andrew Wommack Ministries of Russia. In 2015, the two returned to the States, and Mike serves as vice president of Charis Bible College and International Operations of Andrew Wommack Ministries. Carrie serves as assistant vice president of Charis Bible College and also as the director of the World Outreach Global Training School, one of Charis's third-year vocational schools. She has a heart to reach the world with the grace message and to see powerful ministers raised up with a Great Commission vision. Mike and Carrie have two children, Elliana and Michael—their "missionaries in training."

Greg Mohr

Greg Mohr is director of Charis Bible College in Woodland Park, Colorado. He is also a conference speaker and author and served as senior pastor of River of Life Church in Decatur, Texas, for twenty-four years. He is a graduate of Rhema Bible Training Center in Broken Arrow, Oklahoma, and has earned a master's degree in leadership from Southwestern

Christian University in Bethany, Oklahoma. Greg is married to his best friend, Janice. Together they have four children and eleven grandchildren. Find out more about Greg at **GregMohr.com**.

Duane Sheriff

Duane Sheriff is the senior and founding pastor of Victory Life Church, a multi-campus church headquartered in Durant, Oklahoma. Pastor Duane travels around the world speaking at conferences and churches, as well as Charis Bible College, and has written a number of books. Pastor Duane emphasizes the grace of God and the importance of believers cultivating a personal relationship with the Lord. He is gifted with an anointing and ability to communicate the simplicity of the Gospel. Find out more about Duane at **PastorDuane.com**.

ENDNOTES

1. "How Porn Changes the Brain," *Fight the New Drug*, August 23, 2017, https://fightthenewdrug.org/how-porn-changes-the-brain/.

2. Matthew Wills, "Ernst Röhm, The Highest-Ranking Gay Nazi," JSTOR Daily, March 27, 2017, https://daily.jstor.org/ernst-rohm-the-highest-ranking-gay-nazi/.

3. Jeremy W. Peters, "The Decline of the H Word," *The New York Times*, March 21, 2014, https://www.nytimes.com/2014/03/23/fashion/gays-lesbians-the-term-homosexual.html.

4. Alan P. Bell and Martin S. Weinberg, *Homosexualities: A Study of Diversity Among Men and Women*, (New York, Simon and Schuster, 1978), 308.

5. Paul Cameron, Kirk Cameron, and William L. Playfair, "Does Homosexual Activity Shorten Life?" *Psychological Reports*, Volume 83, Issue 3, 847–866. https://doi.org/10.2466/pr0.1998.83.3.847.

6. Jody L. Herman, Taylor N.T. Brown, and Ann P. Haas, "Suicide Thoughts and Attempts Among Transgender Adults: Findings from the 2015 U.S. Transgender Survey," *Williams Institute of Law*, September 2019, https://williamsinstitute.law.ucla.edu/wp-content/uploads/AFSP-Williams-Suicide-Report-Final.pdf.

7. "Difference Between Transgender and Transsexual," *DifferenceBetween.net*, http://www.differencebetween.net/science/ difference-between-transgender-and-transsexual/.

8. Jan Hoffman, "Estimate of U.S. Transgender Population Doubles to 1.4 Million Adults," *The New York Times*, July 1, 2016, https://www. nytimes.com/2016/07/01/health/transgender-population.html.

9. Kirk Durston, "Why Sexual Morality May Be Far More Important Than You Ever Thought," *Thoughts About God, Truth, and Beauty*, December 1, 2019 https://www.kirkdurston.com/blog/unwin.

10. Colin M. Wright and Emma N. Hilton, "The Dangerous Denial of Sex," *Wall Street Journal*, February 13, 2020, https://www.wsj.com/articles/ the-dangerous-denial-of-sex-11581638089.

CONTACT INFORMATION

Andrew Wommack Ministries, Inc.
PO Box 3333
Colorado Springs, CO 80934-3333
info@awmi.net
awmi.net

Helpline: 719-635-1111 (available 24/7)

Charis Bible College
info@charisbiblecollege.org
844-360-9577
CharisBibleCollege.org

For a complete list of our offices, visit
awmi.net/contact-us.

Connect with us on social media.